AMAZON ECHO DOT (Newest Model) User Guide

The Complete Beginner to Expert Manual for Setting Up, Using, and Getting the Most Out of Your Smart Speaker

Richard Allen

Disclaimer

This book is an independent biographical work and is not authorized, endorsed, or affiliated with Glennon Doyle, his management, or any related entities. While every effort has been made to ensure the accuracy of the information presented, this work is based on publicly available sources, interviews, performances, and commentary. Any errors or omissions are unintentional.

The content reflects the author's interpretations and opinions and is intended for informational and educational purposes only. Names, events, and quotes are used in good faith and for the purpose of documenting and analyzing the subject's career and cultural impact.

Readers are encouraged to consult original sources, official media, and verified interviews for further context.

Contents

Introduction

In an era defined by convenience, connectivity, and voice-driven technology, the Amazon Echo Dot has emerged as a popular gateway into the world of smart living. Compact yet powerful, it combines the functionality of a smart speaker, a virtual assistant, and a control hub for your digital ecosystem. Whether you are a technology enthusiast or a first-time user venturing into the smart home landscape, the Echo Dot promises to streamline your daily tasks, enhance entertainment experiences, and redefine the way you interact with your environment.

With every new iteration, the Echo Dot becomes more refined—offering better performance, improved sound quality, and a more intuitive user interface. The newest model continues this trend, adding enhancements that respond to user needs and feedback. Before exploring the device in depth, it is important to understand what the Echo Dot actually is, why smart speakers have gained widespread popularity, and what distinguishes the latest model from its predecessors.

What Is the Echo Dot?

The Echo Dot is a voice-controlled smart speaker developed by Amazon. It is part of the larger Echo family, which includes a range of devices powered by Amazon's virtual assistant, Alexa. Designed to be compact and affordable, the Echo Dot offers a practical entry point into the world of voice technology and home automation.

At its core, the Echo Dot is built to listen for voice commands and execute tasks using Alexa. These tasks may include checking the weather, setting reminders, playing music, controlling smart home devices, answering questions, or even making hands-free calls. The device includes a built-in speaker, microphones, a processor for handling commands, and a connection to cloud services through Wi-Fi.

The Echo Dot is typically used in individual rooms as a standalone assistant or as part of a larger Echo ecosystem. Users may place one in the bedroom to serve as an alarm clock, another in the kitchen to help with recipes and timers, and yet another in the living room for music and smart home control. Its small size belies its capabilities, and it functions seamlessly with other Echo devices for a synchronized, multi-room experience.

One of the reasons the Echo Dot stands out in the smart speaker market is its balance of affordability and functionality. While some smart speakers prioritize premium sound and aesthetics, the Echo Dot focuses on accessibility, making voice assistant technology widely available to everyday users.

Key Benefits of Using a Smart Speaker

The rise of smart speakers like the Echo Dot reflects broader shifts in how people engage with technology. Rather than typing, tapping, or swiping, users are increasingly turning to voice-based interaction as a more natural, efficient mode of communication with their devices. Below are several core benefits that highlight the appeal of smart speakers:

Hands-Free   Convenience
Smart speakers offer true hands-free control. Whether you're cooking, cleaning, or simply multitasking, the ability to issue voice commands without interrupting your activity is a major advantage. You can ask Alexa to set a timer, play a podcast, turn off the lights, or send a message—all without lifting a finger.

Integrated   Smart   Home   Control
Smart speakers serve as central hubs for managing connected devices throughout your home. Through Alexa, users can control compatible smart bulbs, thermostats, locks, cameras, and appliances with simple voice commands. This integration reduces reliance on multiple apps or physical switches and creates a seamless, automated environment.

Instant   Information   and   Assistance
A smart speaker can provide answers to a wide range of questions almost instantly. From checking the weather and traffic conditions to solving math problems or translating words into another language, Alexa transforms the Echo Dot

into an on-demand research assistant that's always listening and ready to help.

Entertainment and Media Access
The Echo Dot supports various media platforms and services, offering easy access to music, audiobooks, radio stations, and podcasts. You can ask Alexa to play your favorite playlist on Amazon Music, stream a station on Spotify, or continue your audiobook on Audible. With multi-room audio support, your content can follow you from room to room.

Routine Management and Productivity
The Echo Dot is also a personal assistant in the truest sense. It helps organize your life by managing calendars, reminders, to-do lists, and alarms. You can create daily routines that trigger multiple actions with a single command. For example, saying "Alexa, good morning" could turn on the lights, read the news, and start the coffee maker.

Accessibility and Inclusivity
Voice-activated technology can be particularly valuable for individuals with disabilities or mobility challenges. For those who find touchscreens or physical interfaces difficult to use, a smart speaker provides an intuitive, voice-based alternative that enhances independence and control.

Constant Improvement Through Updates
Unlike traditional appliances, smart speakers continually evolve through over-the-air software updates. Amazon frequently adds new features, integrations, and Alexa

skills—meaning that your Echo Dot improves over time without requiring new hardware.

Overview of What's New in the Latest Model

With each release, Amazon refines the Echo Dot's hardware and software to reflect advances in technology and respond to user expectations. The newest Echo Dot (5th Generation) introduces several key upgrades over the previous models, making it the most capable version yet.

Improved   Audio   Performance
The most noticeable enhancement is in sound quality. The 5th Generation Echo Dot includes a redesigned speaker driver that delivers clearer vocals, deeper bass, and overall improved clarity. Whether you're listening to music, podcasts, or voice responses, the sound is richer and more dynamic than ever before.

Amazon has increased the size of the front-firing speaker while refining the acoustic architecture. As a result, the latest Echo Dot offers room-filling audio despite its small footprint. This makes it more suitable for entertainment purposes and everyday listening.

Temperature   Sensor   Integration
One of the more functional additions is the built-in temperature sensor. This allows the Echo Dot to measure the ambient temperature of the room and respond accordingly.

For example, you can create routines where Alexa adjusts your smart thermostat or sends an alert when a certain temperature threshold is reached.

This feature is particularly useful for automating climate control in smart homes and adds another layer of contextual awareness to the device.

Tap-to-Control   Feature

The latest model introduces a tap-to-control function. In addition to voice commands, users can now tap the top of the device to pause music, snooze alarms, or end calls. This tactile option enhances usability for moments when speaking aloud is impractical or disruptive.

Faster   Alexa   Responses

The updated model includes a new AZ2 Neural Edge processor, which allows Alexa to process some voice commands locally instead of relying entirely on cloud-based processing. This leads to faster response times for certain actions, such as controlling lights or checking the time.

Local processing not only improves speed but also enhances privacy, as fewer commands need to be sent to the cloud.

Refined   Design   and   Build

While retaining its spherical form introduced in earlier models, the newest Echo Dot features slight refinements in texture and design. The fabric covering is more durable and visually appealing, and the device is available in new color options such as Deep Sea Blue, which helps it blend more naturally into various home interiors.

The LED indicator ring remains at the base, offering visual feedback without being intrusive. This minimal, modern aesthetic is consistent with Amazon's goal of making the Echo Dot a natural part of the home environment rather than a disruptive piece of technology.

Enhanced   Eero   Integration
Another important addition is Eero Built-in functionality. The Echo Dot (5th Gen) can now function as a Wi-Fi extender for compatible Eero mesh networks, adding up to 1,000 square feet of coverage. This dual-purpose capability transforms the device into a network-strengthening tool, ideal for larger homes or areas with weak signal zones.

Sustainability   Improvements
Amazon has also made efforts to improve the Echo Dot's environmental footprint. The latest model is made from 100% post-consumer recycled fabric and 95% recycled aluminum. It also uses low-power modes and comes in packaging that is fully recyclable.

These sustainability efforts are part of Amazon's broader climate pledge, reflecting growing consumer interest in eco-friendly technology.

As these improvements illustrate, the Echo Dot is not a static product—it is a continually evolving platform that adapts to the changing needs of users and advances in technology. Whether you are upgrading from an older model or using an Echo Dot for the first time, the latest generation offers a more responsive, functional, and immersive experience than ever before.

In the chapters ahead, this guide will walk you through the complete setup process, help you navigate its most powerful features, and offer tips to make the most of your Echo Dot. From basic configuration to advanced routines and integrations, every section is designed to help you unlock the full potential of this compact yet powerful device.

Unboxing and Setup

Bringing home a new Amazon Echo Dot is the first step toward transforming your space into a smarter, more responsive environment. However, before the device can begin working for you, it must be properly unpacked, set up, and configured. This chapter provides a comprehensive guide to unboxing the Echo Dot, understanding its design enhancements, and completing the initial setup process so that it's fully ready for use.

What's Included in the Box

When you open the Echo Dot packaging, you'll find that Amazon continues to emphasize simplicity and minimalism in both design and presentation. The contents are few, but each item plays a critical role in getting your device ready for operation.

Here is what is typically included in the box:

1. **Amazon Echo Dot (Newest Model)** The device itself is spherical, compact, and wrapped in a protective sleeve to prevent scratches during transit.

2. **Power Adapter (15W)** A white or black power adapter (depending on the color of your device), which connects to the Echo

Dot via a proprietary barrel plug. Note that the Echo Dot must remain plugged in to function—there is no internal battery.

3. **Quick Start Guide**
A small booklet offering a concise overview of how to plug in, connect to Wi-Fi, and use Alexa. While this guide covers the basics, this book will provide far more comprehensive instructions.

4. **Warranty and Safety Information**
This includes warranty terms, customer service contacts, and important safety guidelines for using the Echo Dot indoors.

That is the full inventory. Amazon has opted to reduce waste and packaging, so you won't find additional accessories or clutter. If you require items such as wall mounts or protective covers, those must be purchased separately.

Physical Design and Changes from Previous Models

The Echo Dot has undergone notable physical transformations over the years, and the newest model continues this evolution in both form and function. Here is a closer look at how the design of the current generation differs from its predecessors.

Spherical Form Factor

The Echo Dot's shift from a puck-shaped disc (seen in 2nd and 3rd generations) to a sphere began with the 4th generation and continues with the latest model. The spherical design is not only more modern but also more acoustically efficient. The shape helps improve sound projection, allowing for a fuller 360-degree audio experience.

Refined Fabric Exterior

The fabric mesh that covers the device is tighter and more durable in the latest model. It is available in updated color options such as **Charcoal**, **Glacier White**, and **Deep Sea Blue**, giving users more flexibility to match home decor. The fabric material improves the device's aesthetics and contributes to better sound diffusion.

LED Light Ring at the Base

Earlier Echo Dots had the LED ring on the top surface, circling the outer edge of the flat top. In the current version, the ring has been moved to the base. This change not only provides a more subtle, ambient glow but also reflects off surfaces, making it more visible when the device is on a shelf or desk.

The LED ring serves multiple purposes—it lights up in blue when Alexa is listening, pulses yellow for notifications, turns red when the microphone is muted, and glows green for calls or Drop In interactions.

Tap-to-Control Functionality

One of the physical usability enhancements in the newest model is the **tap-to-control** feature. With a light tap on the top of the device, you can:

- Pause or resume music

- Snooze alarms

- End calls This adds an extra layer of manual interaction for times when voice control is not ideal.

Hidden Microphones and Speaker Grille

The array of microphones is subtly integrated into the surface of the device to maintain its clean aesthetic. These microphones use far-field voice recognition to pick up your commands even when music is playing or you are across the room.

The speaker grille is integrated seamlessly into the fabric mesh, allowing for an unobtrusive appearance while housing a 1.73-inch front-firing speaker. The result is clearer audio with more defined bass compared to earlier versions.

Rear Ports

The back of the Echo Dot contains a power port and, unlike some earlier models, no 3.5mm audio output. This is a deliberate move by Amazon to simplify the device, although it does remove the option of connecting the Echo Dot directly to external speakers via AUX cable.

Step-by-Step Setup Process

Once the Echo Dot is unboxed and plugged in, the setup process begins. Amazon has made the process straightforward, but it requires a few key steps, including connecting to Wi-Fi and configuring settings via the Alexa mobile app. Follow this step-by-step guide to ensure a smooth setup.

Step 1: Plug in the Echo Dot

1. Connect the included power adapter to the port at the back of the device.

2. Plug the adapter into a wall outlet.

3. The light ring will illuminate blue, then orange. The orange light indicates that the Echo Dot is in **setup mode**.

Step 2: Download and Launch the Alexa App

1. On your smartphone or tablet, go to the App Store (iOS) or Google Play Store (Android).

2. Search for **"Amazon Alexa"** and install the official app.

3. Open the Alexa app and sign in using your Amazon account credentials. If you do not already have an Amazon account, you will need to create one.

Step 3: Add a New Device

17

1. Once logged in, tap the "**Devices**" icon in the bottom navigation bar.

2. Tap the "+" icon in the top right corner.

3. Select "**Add Device**" from the menu.

4. Choose "**Amazon Echo**" > "**Echo Dot.**"

Step 4: Connect Echo Dot to Wi-Fi

1. The app will begin searching for devices in setup mode. Ensure your Echo Dot is powered on and the light ring is orange.

2. Once the app detects the device, tap on it to begin configuration.

3. Select your Wi-Fi network from the list displayed in the app.

4. Enter your Wi-Fi password when prompted.

5. The Echo Dot will attempt to connect. When successful, the light ring will briefly turn blue and then go off, indicating readiness.

Step 5: Customize Device Settings

After connecting to Wi-Fi, the app will walk you through the following customization options:

- **Device Name**: You can give your Echo Dot a unique name (e.g., "Bedroom Dot" or "Kitchen Assistant").

- **Room/Group Assignment**: Assign the device to a room (such as Living Room, Office, etc.) for easier control when using multiple Echo devices.

- **Location**: Enter your zip code or address for localized services (weather, traffic updates).

- **Time Zone**: Set the correct time zone for alarms and reminders to function accurately.

Step 6: Enable Voice Recognition

The app may prompt you to enable **Voice ID** and **Alexa Voice Profiles**. This feature allows Alexa to recognize different users by their voice and deliver personalized responses such as individual calendars, playlists, and reminders.

Step 7: Review Privacy and Permissions

The Alexa app will present options to review and configure privacy settings. You can:

- Mute the microphone manually (physical button on the device)

- Review voice recordings

- Enable or disable features like Drop In

- Adjust how long Alexa stores your data

It is recommended to visit **Settings > Alexa Privacy** in the app and familiarize yourself with available privacy controls.

Step 8: Link Music and Media Services

To make the most of your Echo Dot, you should link your favorite media accounts:

- Navigate to **Settings > Music & Podcasts**

- Link accounts such as Amazon Music, Spotify, Apple Music, Pandora, or TuneIn

- Set a default service so Alexa uses your preferred platform without prompting

You can also connect services for:

- News briefings

- Smart home control

- Calendar and email access

Step 9: Test the Echo Dot

After setup, try a few sample commands to verify everything is working:

- "Alexa, what's the weather today?"

- "Alexa, play jazz music."

- "Alexa, set a timer for 10 minutes."

- "Alexa, what time is it?"

If Alexa responds appropriately, your device is set up successfully and ready for regular use.

Step 10: Install Software Updates

Amazon devices typically update automatically, but you can manually check for updates by saying:

- "Alexa, check for software updates."

The device may restart during the process. Keeping the Echo Dot updated ensures optimal performance and access to the latest features.

Navigating the Alexa App

The Amazon Alexa app is the command center of your Echo Dot and all compatible smart devices in your ecosystem. While the Echo Dot can respond to voice commands on its own, the app allows for deeper configuration, personalization, and control. Understanding how to use the Alexa app is essential to getting the most out of your smart speaker.

Whether you're adjusting settings, linking accounts, creating routines, or managing groups of devices, the app offers the tools necessary to tailor your Alexa experience. This chapter provides an in-depth overview of installing the Alexa app, navigating its key features, customizing preferences, and organizing your devices for efficiency and ease of use.

How to Install and Use the App

Before interacting with your Echo Dot, the first essential step is installing the Alexa app. The app acts as the interface between you, your Amazon account, and the Echo ecosystem.

Installation Steps

1. **Download the App**

   o For iOS users: Open the App Store and search for **"Amazon Alexa."**

   o For Android users: Open Google Play Store and search for **"Amazon Alexa."**

   o Select the official app by Amazon and tap **Install**.

2. **Open and Sign In**

   o Once installed, open the app.

   o Sign in using your **Amazon account credentials**. If you don't have an Amazon account, the app will prompt you to create one before proceeding.

3. **Permissions and Notifications**

   o Upon first use, the app will request permissions for microphone access, location services, and notifications.

   o Grant the necessary permissions to enable full functionality (e.g., calling, weather updates, location-specific routines).

Main Navigation Menu

Upon successful login, the home screen displays cards such as recent interactions, weather, and suggestions. The bottom navigation bar includes five core sections:

- **Home**: Displays personalized content, including recent Alexa activity, suggestions, and tips.

- **Communicate**: Used for messaging, calling, Drop In, and announcements.

- **Play**: Gives access to media content—music, podcasts, audiobooks.

- **Devices**: The control hub for managing Echo speakers, smart home gadgets, and groups.

- **More**: Contains account settings, routines, lists, skills, and app preferences.

Navigating between these tabs is intuitive, with clear icons and labels. Each tab opens to its own set of features, many of which can be expanded by tapping sub-menus or device-specific settings.

Customizing Settings and Preferences

One of the Alexa app's most powerful features is the ability to personalize how Alexa behaves. This section covers key customization areas to enhance functionality and user experience.

Personal Preferences

To access your settings:

1. Tap **More** in the bottom navigation bar.

2. Select **Settings** from the menu.

From here, you can configure:

- **Your Profile**: Add your name, email, voice ID, and communication preferences.

- **Alexa Voice Responses**: Choose between standard, brief, or whisper mode for replies.

- **App Notifications**: Control which types of alerts (e.g., reminders, announcements) appear on your phone.

- **Units and Measurements**: Select temperature in Celsius or Fahrenheit, and choose 12-hour or 24-hour time format.

Voice Recognition and Voice ID

Setting up **Voice ID** allows Alexa to recognize individual voices and tailor responses accordingly. Each household member can create their own profile and enjoy personalized features such as:

- Music playlists

- Calendar access

- Call and message history

- Shopping lists

To enable Voice ID:

1. Go to **Settings > Your Profile & Family**.

2. Select **Add Your Voice**.

3. Follow the voice prompts to train Alexa to recognize you.

This feature helps Alexa distinguish between users and provide a more personalized experience in multi-user households.

Alexa Skills

Skills are third-party applications that extend Alexa's capabilities, much like apps do for smartphones. There are skills for games, fitness, education, home automation, productivity, and more.

To browse or enable skills:

1. Tap **More > Skills & Games**.

2. Use the search bar or browse categories to discover new skills.

3. Tap on a skill, then tap **Enable to Use**.

4. Some skills may require account linking (e.g., Spotify, Uber).

Enabled skills are immediately available to your Echo Dot. You can manage them by visiting **Your Skills** within the Skills section.

Wake Word and Language

By default, the wake word is **"Alexa"**, but you can change it to **"Amazon,"** **"Echo,"** or **"Computer"** if desired. To modify:

1. Go to **Devices > Echo & Alexa**.

2. Select your Echo Dot.

3. Tap **Device Settings > Wake Word**.

4. Choose from the available options.

Similarly, you can set the device language from a list of supported options. This is especially useful for bilingual households or users more comfortable in languages other than English.

Privacy Controls

Amazon includes detailed privacy settings accessible via:

More > Settings > Alexa Privacy

Key features include:

- **Review Voice History**: Listen to or delete recorded interactions.

- **Manage Skill Permissions**: Control which skills can access personal data.

- **Mute the Microphone**: A hardware button on the Echo Dot disables all listening temporarily.

- **Voice Deletion Commands**: You can also say, "Alexa, delete what I just said," or "Alexa, delete everything I said today."

Privacy controls empower users to manage how their data is used and provide transparency in how Alexa interacts with them.

Managing Devices and Groups

The Alexa app not only controls your Echo Dot, but it also serves as the central hub for managing all connected smart home devices. Whether you have multiple Echo speakers or a full range of smart devices—lights, thermostats, plugs, cameras—the **Devices** tab is where all management occurs.

Adding a New Device

To add a new smart device:

1. Go to **Devices**.

2. Tap the "+" icon in the top-right corner.

3. Select **Add Device**.

4. Choose the device type or brand (e.g., light bulb, plug, thermostat).

5. Follow the manufacturer's instructions for pairing mode, then complete the setup through the app.

Many popular brands (e.g., Philips Hue, TP-Link, Ring) offer Alexa compatibility. For devices requiring account linking, the app will guide you through the process.

Echo Device Management

Each Echo device, including your Dot, can be managed individually:

1. Tap **Devices > Echo & Alexa**.

2. Select the Echo Dot you want to configure.

From this menu, you can:

- Change the wake word

- Adjust volume and sound settings

- Rename the device

- View Wi-Fi details

- Set location and time zone

- Enable Do Not Disturb mode

- Manage connected skills and routines

These options help maintain control and consistency, especially if you own multiple Echo devices.

Creating Device Groups

Device grouping allows you to control multiple devices at once with a single command. For instance, saying "Alexa, turn off the bedroom" can deactivate the smart light, fan, and TV all at once—if they are grouped accordingly.

To create a group:

1. Tap **Devices**.

2. Tap **"+"** > **Add Group**.

3. Choose a predefined name (e.g., Living Room) or enter a custom name.

4. Select devices to include in the group.

5. Tap **Save**.

Now, Alexa can control that group with a single voice command.

Multi-Room Music Groups

The Alexa app also allows you to set up **Multi-Room Music** groups to synchronize audio playback across multiple Echo devices.

To create one:

1. Tap **Devices**.

2. Select + > **Set Up Multi-Room Music**.

3. Choose a name for your speaker group (e.g., "Everywhere").

4. Select all the Echo devices to include.

5. Tap **Save**.

Once created, say, "Alexa, play music on [group name]," and all selected speakers will stream audio in unison.

Device Routines and Automation

Within the Alexa app, you can build **Routines**, which are sequences of actions triggered by a single voice command, time, or sensor event.

To set one up:

1. Tap **More > Routines**.

2. Tap the "+" to create a new routine.

3. Choose a **Trigger** (e.g., voice command, scheduled time, sensor).

4. Select **Actions** (e.g., turn on lights, play music, provide weather report).

5. Choose the device that should respond.

6. Tap **Save**.

Example: A "Good Morning" routine could read your calendar, turn on lights, start a playlist, and provide the weather—all from one command.

Routines are powerful tools for automating daily habits and creating a cohesive smart home experience.

Voice Commands and Everyday Use

The true utility of the Amazon Echo Dot lies in its ability to understand and execute spoken commands. Powered by Alexa, Amazon's intelligent voice assistant, the device transforms everyday interactions into seamless voice-driven experiences. Whether you're checking the weather, setting an alarm, streaming music, or controlling your lights, the Echo Dot simplifies these tasks with minimal effort.

This chapter explores how to effectively use voice commands for daily tasks. It provides a detailed breakdown of common interactions, media consumption, productivity features, and smart home control. Mastery of these functions will allow you to make the most of your Echo Dot in every room and in virtually every aspect of your daily routine.

Basic Voice Commands

Understanding basic voice commands is the foundation for using the Echo Dot effectively. Each command begins with the **wake word**, typically "Alexa," followed by an instruction. This section outlines essential command categories and examples to get you started.

General Commands

These are simple, day-to-day queries that showcase Alexa's core capabilities.

- "Alexa, what time is it?"

- "Alexa, what's the date today?"

- "Alexa, what's the weather like?"

- "Alexa, tell me a joke."

- "Alexa, how do you spell 'necessary'?"

- "Alexa, flip a coin."

These examples illustrate how Alexa responds to informational requests, casual inquiries, or entertainment-related prompts.

Communication

You can use Alexa to initiate calls, send messages, or announce something to all Echo devices in your home.

- "Alexa, call John."

- "Alexa, send a message to Emma."

- "Alexa, drop in on the kitchen."

- "Alexa, announce 'Dinner is ready!'"

These features require device permissions and setup within the Alexa app, particularly contact syncing and Drop In permissions.

Device Interaction

You can control Alexa itself with a few helpful commands:

- "Alexa, stop."

- "Alexa, volume up."

- "Alexa, volume 5." (Set between 1–10)

- "Alexa, what did you just say?"

- "Alexa, repeat."

These commands help you fine-tune interactions and keep the experience responsive and intuitive.

Using Alexa for Timers, Reminders, and Alarms

One of the Echo Dot's most practical applications is task management—especially with time-based features. These tools are especially useful in the kitchen, bedroom, office, or during routines when hands-free control is critical.

Timers

Timers are useful for cooking, exercising, studying, or any task that requires countdown tracking.

- "Alexa, set a timer for 20 minutes."

- "Alexa, set a pasta timer for 8 minutes."

- "Alexa, how much time is left on my timer?"

- "Alexa, cancel the pasta timer."

Alexa supports multiple timers at once, each of which can be named for clarity. This is particularly valuable in multi-tasking environments like the kitchen.

Alarms

Alarms are ideal for waking up, taking medication, or setting recurring time cues.

- "Alexa, set an alarm for 6:30 AM."

- "Alexa, set a repeating alarm for weekdays at 7:00 AM."

- "Alexa, snooze."

- "Alexa, cancel my 6:30 alarm."

Alarms can include custom sounds, and you can change the alarm tone from the Alexa app under **Device Settings > Sounds**.

Reminders

Reminders provide personalized alerts for important events or tasks. They can be set for specific times or locations (via the Alexa app on mobile).

- "Alexa, remind me to take out the trash at 8 PM."

- "Alexa, remind me to call Mom tomorrow at noon."

- "Alexa, what are my reminders?"

- "Alexa, delete my 8 PM reminder."

Reminders are ideal for habit building, daily tasks, or appointments that need timely prompts.

Music, News, Weather, and Podcasts

Echo Dot users often rely on the device for media consumption. Alexa supports multiple streaming services and provides voice-accessible entertainment and information throughout the day.

Music

The Echo Dot is compatible with Amazon Music, Spotify, Apple Music, Pandora, iHeartRadio, and other services. Once your preferred platform is linked in the Alexa app, you can begin playback by voice.

- "Alexa, play jazz."

- "Alexa, play my workout playlist."

- "Alexa, play Taylor Swift on Spotify."

- "Alexa, shuffle songs by The Beatles."

- "Alexa, pause the music."

- "Alexa, what song is this?"

If you have multiple Echo devices, you can also say:

- "Alexa, play music everywhere," to initiate synchronized playback across all speakers in your home.

You can control playback volume, skip tracks, and repeat songs all through voice commands.

News

Alexa can deliver news updates in various formats, including briefings from global and regional news outlets. Customize your Flash Briefing or default news service in the Alexa app under **Settings > News**.

- "Alexa, what's in the news?"

- "Alexa, play my Flash Briefing."

- "Alexa, give me the latest from BBC News."

Alexa can read both headlines and full reports depending on your chosen source. You can also enable additional news skills for region-specific content.

Weather

One of the most frequently used voice commands is checking the weather.

- "Alexa, what's the weather today?"

- "Alexa, will it rain this weekend?"

- "Alexa, what's the weather in New York tomorrow?"

- "Alexa, do I need an umbrella?"

You can also ask for weather forecasts for up to 10 days in advance or ask about specific parameters like wind speed, humidity, and UV index.

Podcasts and Audiobooks

For spoken-word content, Alexa supports popular podcast services like Apple Podcasts, Spotify, and TuneIn, as well as audiobooks from Audible.

- "Alexa, play the latest episode of 'The Daily.'"

- "Alexa, resume my Audible book."

- "Alexa, play a podcast about health."

- "Alexa, skip ahead 30 seconds."

These features are valuable for learning, relaxation, or entertainment while multitasking, commuting, or unwinding.

Controlling Smart Home Devices

The Echo Dot acts as a central hub for compatible smart home devices. With Alexa, you can control lights, thermostats, plugs, cameras, locks, and more—all with your voice.

Smart Lights

After pairing your smart bulbs through the Alexa app, you can issue voice commands such as:

- "Alexa, turn on the living room lights."

- "Alexa, dim the bedroom lights to 30%."

- "Alexa, change the kitchen lights to blue."

- "Alexa, turn off all the lights."

Alexa allows you to group devices (e.g., "Kitchen," "Bedroom") and apply commands universally or by zone.

Smart Plugs and Appliances

Smart plugs enable Alexa to control non-smart devices like coffee makers, fans, or lamps.

- "Alexa, turn on the coffee maker."

- "Alexa, turn off the heater."

- "Alexa, is the fan on?"

Once named and grouped, you can automate routines such as "Alexa, good night," to turn off all connected plugs and lights.

Thermostats

Alexa-compatible thermostats allow temperature control and schedule management by voice:

- "Alexa, set the thermostat to 72 degrees."

- "Alexa, what's the temperature in the living room?"

- "Alexa, increase the temperature by 2 degrees."

You can also include temperature adjustments in routines—for example, reducing heat at night.

Security Devices

Alexa integrates with smart locks, doorbells, and cameras from brands like Ring, August, Arlo, and Blink.

- "Alexa, show the front door camera." (requires Echo Show or Fire TV)

- "Alexa, lock the back door."

- "Alexa, is the garage door closed?"

Security device integration enables hands-free monitoring and access, especially valuable when you're away or occupied.

Automation and Routines

For advanced smart home management, Alexa routines allow you to trigger multiple actions with one command:

- "Alexa, good morning" could:
    o Turn on the lights
    o Start the coffee maker
    o Read the weather
    o Play your morning news briefing

To build routines:

1. Open the Alexa app
2. Tap **More > Routines**
3. Create a trigger (voice, time, or device state)
4. Add actions like smart device control, weather, news, volume adjustment

These routines can be personalized per user and room, optimizing your home environment based on your habits and preferences.

Advanced Features

While basic commands and daily functions make the Echo Dot immediately useful, its advanced features significantly enhance its value. Beyond simply responding to your voice, Alexa can anticipate your needs, streamline communication within the home, provide synchronized audio experiences, and offer granular control over your privacy.

This chapter explains how to make the most of advanced capabilities such as Alexa Routines and automation, in-home communication tools like Drop In and Announcements, multi-room audio configuration, and the robust privacy settings available to help users maintain control of their data and device behavior.

Alexa Routines and Automation

One of the most powerful features of Alexa is its ability to automate a series of actions based on a single command, a scheduled time, or a trigger from a smart home sensor. These are known as **Routines**.

Routines transform your Echo Dot from a reactive assistant into a proactive tool that integrates seamlessly into your daily life. You can create a routine to start your morning, signal bedtime, enhance productivity, or set the mood in your home.

Creating a Routine

To create a routine, follow these steps in the Alexa app:

1. Open the app and tap **More** on the bottom navigation bar.

2. Select **Routines**.

3. Tap the "+" icon in the top right corner.

4. Choose:

    o **Enter routine name**: Name the routine (e.g., "Morning Routine").

    o **When this happens**: Select a trigger such as a voice command ("Alexa, good morning"), a time of day, or a device action (e.g., a motion sensor detects movement).

    o **Add action**: Choose one or more actions to perform. These may include:

        ▪ Turning on smart lights

        ▪ Adjusting thermostat temperature

        ▪ Playing music or radio

        ▪ Reading the weather or news

- Sending announcements or reminders

5. Choose the Echo device(s) that will perform the routine.

6. Tap **Save**.

Your routine is now ready to use.

Example Routines

Morning Routine:

- Trigger: 7:00 AM, every weekday

- Actions:

  o Turn on bedroom lights

  o Provide weather forecast

  o Start "Daily Mix" playlist on Spotify

  o Announce "Good morning. Time to start your day."

Bedtime Routine:

- Trigger: Voice command "Alexa, good night"

- Actions:

  o Turn off all lights

  o Lower thermostat

o Enable Do Not Disturb

o Play white noise

Home Security Routine:

- Trigger: Smart door sensor detects opening

- Actions:

  o Announce "Front door opened" on all Echo
     devices

  o Turn on hallway lights (at night)

  o Send a notification to your phone

Smart Automation with Sensors

If you have motion sensors or door/window sensors linked
to your Alexa ecosystem, you can create event-based
automation. For example:

- When motion is detected in the hallway between 11
  PM and 6 AM, Alexa can turn on low lighting to help
  navigate in the dark.

This type of automation enhances both convenience and
safety, especially in larger homes or for families with elderly
individuals or children.

Drop In, Announcements, and Calling

Echo devices offer more than voice command and smart control—they also function as an in-home communication system. Alexa supports three primary communication features:

Drop In

Drop In allows for real-time, two-way communication between Echo devices in your home or between authorized contacts.

How to use Drop In:

- Say: "Alexa, drop in on [device name]" (e.g., "Alexa, drop in on the kitchen")

The receiving device will automatically connect, and the audio will begin streaming immediately. This is useful for:

- Checking in on children or elderly family members

- Calling someone to dinner

- Monitoring another room without needing to shout

To enable Drop In:

1. Open the Alexa app.

2. Tap **Devices > Echo & Alexa**.

3. Choose a device, then go to **Communications > Drop In**.

4. Select **On**, **Only my household**, or **Off**.

You can also enable Drop In for specific contacts through the **Communicate** tab in the app. Only approved contacts can use Drop In, which adds a layer of security and consent.

Announcements

Announcements send one-way voice messages to all Echo devices in your home at once.

Say:

- "Alexa, announce 'It's time to leave for school.'"

- "Alexa, tell everyone dinner is ready."

Every Echo device will play the announcement with a chime and your message. This feature mimics a home intercom system and is ideal for quick, broadcast-style communication.

You can also type announcements in the Alexa app by going to **Communicate > Announce**, entering your message, and choosing the devices to broadcast to.

Calling and Messaging

Alexa supports calling and messaging to other Alexa users and phone contacts. This feature includes:

- Alexa-to-Alexa calling (Echo to Echo)

- Calling mobile and landline numbers in supported regions

- Sending voice or text messages

Say:

- "Alexa, call Dad."

- "Alexa, message Sarah."

- "Alexa, answer the call."

To set up calling:

1. Open the Alexa app.

2. Tap **Communicate > Call**.

3. Grant permissions to access your contacts.

4. Verify your phone number.

Once set up, Alexa can use voice recognition to identify which user is speaking and call the correct contact.

You can view and manage contacts under **Communicate > Contacts** in the Alexa app.

Multi-Room Audio Setup

The Echo Dot is an excellent music player on its own, but it becomes significantly more powerful when part of a **multi-**

room audio system. This allows users to synchronize music across multiple Echo devices throughout the home.

Setting Up Multi-Room Audio

To create a multi-room music group:

1. Open the Alexa app.

2. Tap **Devices**.

3. Tap + and choose **Set Up Multi-Room Music**.

4. Select a name for your group (e.g., "Everywhere," "Downstairs," "Upstairs").

5. Choose the Echo devices to include in this group.

6. Tap **Save**.

Once configured, you can say:

- "Alexa, play jazz in the living room."

- "Alexa, play pop everywhere."

- "Alexa, stop the music upstairs."

This is especially useful during parties, cleaning routines, or when moving through multiple rooms during the day.

Managing Multi-Room Audio

Within the Alexa app:

51

- You can edit or delete audio groups at any time.

- Adjust volume for individual devices even when grouped.

- Stream different content to different rooms if desired (e.g., podcasts in the office, music in the kitchen).

Alexa also supports stereo pairing of two Echo Dots (same generation), allowing them to act as left and right speakers for enhanced audio performance. Pairing must be done through **Devices > Echo & Alexa > [Device] > Stereo Pair/Subwoofer**.

Privacy Settings and Microphone Control

Privacy and security are essential considerations when using a voice-activated device. Amazon has implemented multiple layers of control to allow users to manage their data and limit device access.

Microphone Control

Every Echo Dot includes a physical **microphone mute button**. When pressed:

- The LED ring turns red.

- The device stops listening for the wake word.

- Alexa will not respond until the microphone is re-enabled.

This manual option provides immediate privacy when needed.

You can also say:

- "Alexa, mute yourself."

- "Alexa, stop listening."

Note: These voice commands only temporarily suspend listening and may not replace the mute button's function, depending on the device.

Alexa Privacy Dashboard

To manage voice recordings and data preferences, go to: **More > Settings > Alexa Privacy**

Key options include:

- **Review Voice History**: View, listen to, or delete previous voice commands.

- **Delete Recordings Automatically**: Choose to delete recordings after 3 or 18 months, or not at all.

- **Voice Deletion Commands**: Enable commands such as:

    o "Alexa, delete what I just said."

- o "Alexa, delete everything I said today."

- **Manage Smart Home Device History**: Delete data related to smart device interactions.

- **Skill Permissions**: Control which third-party skills can access your location, email, or phone number.

Local Voice Processing

With the latest Echo Dot (5th Generation), some voice processing can be handled locally on the device rather than in the cloud. This means:

- Faster response time for certain commands (like turning on lights).

- Fewer voice interactions being stored or transmitted externally.

This local processing enhancement aligns with Amazon's goal to improve privacy and responsiveness.

Troubleshooting and Maintenance

Even the most reliable devices may occasionally encounter performance issues or require maintenance. The Amazon Echo Dot is designed to operate consistently and efficiently, but users may still experience challenges such as connectivity problems, unresponsive behavior, or difficulties interacting with Alexa. This chapter provides a comprehensive guide to identifying and resolving common issues, performing a full reset if necessary, and ensuring your device is always up to date with the latest software.

By following these troubleshooting and maintenance best practices, you can resolve most technical problems on your own and maintain the Echo Dot's performance over the long term.

Common Issues and How to Fix Them

Below are the most frequently reported issues Echo Dot users encounter, along with step-by-step solutions for each.

1. Alexa Is Not Responding

If Alexa does not acknowledge the wake word or appears unresponsive:

Possible Causes:

- Microphone is muted

- Device lost Wi-Fi connection

- Audio output is too low or disabled

- Alexa servers are temporarily unavailable

Solutions:

- Check that the **microphone button** is not red. Press it once to reactivate listening.

- Say "Alexa" again and watch for the light ring to activate. If it remains dark, ensure the device is plugged in and powered on.

- Verify your Wi-Fi is active. Restart your router if needed.

- Use the Alexa app to test the device's status (navigate to **Devices > Echo & Alexa > [Device]**).

- Try restarting the Echo Dot by unplugging it for 30 seconds, then plugging it back in.

2. Echo Dot Not Connecting to Wi-Fi

Without a stable internet connection, the Echo Dot cannot process commands or perform tasks.

Possible Causes:

- Incorrect Wi-Fi password

- Router is offline or out of range

- Network congestion or interference

- Firmware updates pending

Solutions:

- Reconnect your device to Wi-Fi using the Alexa app:

  1. Open **Devices > Echo & Alexa > [Device]**

  2. Tap **Settings > Wi-Fi Network**

  3. Follow the prompts to connect to the correct network.

- Ensure the Echo Dot is within 30 feet of your router.

- Restart your router and Echo Dot.

- Avoid placing the Echo Dot near microwaves or thick walls, which can disrupt signals.

3. Audio Quality Issues or No Sound

If the Echo Dot produces distorted sound or is silent:

Possible Causes:

- Volume is set too low

- Speaker hardware is malfunctioning

- Bluetooth connection is interfering

- Firmware is outdated

Solutions:

- Say "Alexa, volume 7" to raise the volume.

- Press the physical volume-up button on the device.

- Disconnect Bluetooth:

  o Say "Alexa, disconnect."

  o Open the Alexa app and unpair from **Settings > Bluetooth Devices**.

- Restart the Echo Dot.

- Try playing different audio content to rule out issues with specific apps or services.

4. Alexa Misunderstanding or Mishearing Commands

Occasionally, Alexa may misinterpret your commands or activate unnecessarily.

Possible Causes:

- Wake word triggered by ambient sounds

- Background noise interfering

- User pronunciation variations

Solutions:

- Train your **Voice ID** in the Alexa app for better recognition.

- Move the device away from TVs or loud appliances.

- Change the wake word (Alexa, Amazon, Echo, or Computer) if false triggers occur often.

- Speak clearly and allow a brief pause after saying the wake word.

5. Alexa Skills Not Working

Skills are third-party extensions, and if they stop functioning:

Possible Causes:

- Skill not enabled

- Account link expired

- Outdated skill or app issue

Solutions:

- Open **More > Skills & Games > Your Skills** in the Alexa app.

- Disable and re-enable the skill.

- Re-link any required third-party accounts.

- Try a different skill to verify if the issue is isolated.

6. Bluetooth or Device Pairing Issues

If Echo Dot isn't pairing with other devices:

Possible Causes:

- Device out of range

- Previous connection not cleared

- Bluetooth settings are incorrect

Solutions:

- Say "Alexa, pair" to enter pairing mode.

- On your smartphone or device, search for available Bluetooth connections and select your Echo Dot.

- Clear old pairings via **Settings > Bluetooth Devices** in the Alexa app.

- Restart both devices and attempt pairing again.

7. Echo Dot Freezing or Restarting Frequently

Unexpected reboots or freezing could indicate:

Possible Causes:

- Power supply instability

- Software error

- Overheating

Solutions:

- Ensure you are using the original Amazon power adapter.

- Place the device in a cool, ventilated space.

- Check for software updates (explained later in this chapter).

- Perform a factory reset if the issue persists.

Resetting the Device

If problems persist despite troubleshooting, resetting the Echo Dot can resolve more complex issues. This process restores the device to its factory settings, erasing all custom configurations, linked accounts, and preferences.

When to Reset

- After repeated Wi-Fi failures

- When transferring ownership of the device

- If Alexa becomes unresponsive after multiple reboots

- To fix persistent glitches that software updates cannot resolve

Reset Methods by Generation

For Echo Dot (5th Generation and 4th Generation):

1. Press and hold the **Action button** (the button with a dot) for **20 seconds**.

2. Wait until the **light ring turns orange**, then blue.

3. The device will enter setup mode, confirmed by Alexa saying it's ready for setup.

For Echo Dot with Clock:

Follow the same steps as above. Resetting the device will also remove any time or display settings.

Alternative via Alexa App:

1. Open the Alexa app.

2. Navigate to **Devices > Echo & Alexa > [Your Device]**.

3. Tap **Factory Reset** under **Device Settings**.

Post-Reset Process:

- After resetting, the device must be set up again as if it were new.

- Use the Alexa app to reconnect to Wi-Fi, name the device, and link accounts.

Important Note: Resetting cannot be undone. Ensure you back up any information or preferences you may need.

Keeping Software Updated

To maintain optimal performance and security, Amazon frequently releases software updates for Echo devices. These updates include new features, bug fixes, performance improvements, and compatibility with newly supported devices or services.

Automatic Updates

By default, the Echo Dot downloads and installs software updates automatically when connected to Wi-Fi and not in active use. You typically do not need to manually check for updates.

Indications of an update:

- The device may briefly restart on its own.

- You may notice a slight delay in response immediately after the update.

- Updates generally occur at night or during periods of inactivity.

Manually Checking for Updates

You can force Alexa to check for updates using a voice command:

- "Alexa, check for software updates."

Alternatively, restart the Echo Dot:

1. Unplug it from power.

2. Wait 30 seconds.

3. Plug it back in and wait for the startup cycle.

If an update is available, it will be downloaded during this process.

Verifying the Software Version

To confirm that your Echo Dot is running the latest firmware:

1. Open the Alexa app.

2. Go to **Devices > Echo & Alexa > [Your Device]**.

3. Scroll to the **Device Software Version** section.

Compare the listed version with Amazon's official firmware update page for Echo devices (available on Amazon's Help site).

Tips to Ensure Smooth Updates

- Keep your Echo Dot **connected to a stable Wi-Fi network** at all times.

- Avoid unplugging the device frequently, especially overnight.

- Ensure the power adapter is securely connected and use only official accessories.

Routine Maintenance Best Practices

To ensure the Echo Dot operates reliably over time, consider the following maintenance tips:

Physical Cleaning

- Gently wipe the exterior of the device with a soft, dry microfiber cloth.

- Avoid using any abrasive cleaners or moisture near the power port or microphone.

- If using in a kitchen or dusty environment, periodically clean the speaker grille.

Location and Placement

- Place your Echo Dot at least 8 inches from walls for better sound and microphone reception.

- Avoid placing it directly next to noisy appliances, which can interfere with listening.

- Keep it away from sources of extreme heat or direct sunlight.

Review App Settings Monthly

- Periodically open the Alexa app to check:
    - Routines and scheduled triggers
    - Device groupings
    - Account permissions
    - Connected services (Spotify, smart devices, etc.)

This keeps your setup organized and ensures you're using the latest available features.

Tips and Tricks

The Echo Dot is far more than a voice-activated speaker. With a vast array of third-party integrations, customization options, and intelligent features, users can transform Alexa into a highly personalized assistant. This chapter focuses on lesser-known capabilities that elevate the user experience, including recommended third-party skills, productivity techniques, and features tailored specifically for children and families.

By mastering these advanced applications and configurations, you can take full advantage of your Echo Dot's potential—turning it into a tool for learning, organization, entertainment, and secure family interaction.

Useful Third-Party Skills

Amazon Alexa's capabilities can be extended through **third-party skills**—voice-enabled applications developed by companies and independent developers. These skills allow Alexa to do everything from playing trivia games to controlling fitness apps and tracking shipments.

There are over 100,000 skills available in the Alexa Skills Store. Below are curated categories and standout examples that significantly enhance the Echo Dot experience.

News and Information

Stay informed and entertained with real-time updates and specialized content.

- **NPR News** – "Alexa, play NPR News." Delivers hourly news updates from National Public Radio.

- **TED Talks** – "Alexa, play a TED Talk." Access thousands of talks on science, motivation, technology, and more.

- **The Daily by The New York Times** – "Alexa, play The Daily." Offers in-depth daily news segments on current events.

Productivity and Utility

Boost organization and efficiency with skills designed for reminders, task management, and time tracking.

- **Any.do** – Integrates to-do lists across devices. "Alexa, add 'submit report' to my Any.do list."

- **Trello** – Connects Alexa with your Trello boards for managing projects. "Alexa, add a card to my work board."

- **Big Sky** – A highly detailed weather forecasting skill.

"Alexa, ask Big Sky what the weather will be like this weekend."

Education and Learning

Skills for language learning, general knowledge, and practice quizzes.

- **Duolingo** – Practice language learning with daily drills.
  "Alexa, open Duolingo."

- **Spelling Bee** – A fun spelling quiz game.
  "Alexa, open Spelling Bee."

- **Word of the Day** – Expand your vocabulary.
  "Alexa, what's the word of the day?"

Entertainment and Games

Keep the household entertained with interactive content and voice games.

- **Jeopardy!** – Official trivia game modeled on the popular TV show.
  "Alexa, play Jeopardy!"

- **Escape the Room** – A voice-based escape adventure.
  "Alexa, open Escape the Room."

- **Ambient Sounds** – White noise, ocean waves, rain, and other sounds to help you relax or sleep. "Alexa, play ocean sounds."

Smart Home Integration

Expand your Echo Dot's smart home control with brand-specific skills.

- **Philips Hue** – For lighting control. "Alexa, dim the living room lights to 30%."

- **Nest Thermostat** – Manage your thermostat by voice.
  "Alexa, set the temperature to 72 degrees."

- **Ring** – Access Ring video doorbells and security systems.
  "Alexa, show me the front door."

To enable a skill:

1. Open the Alexa app.

2. Tap **More > Skills & Games**.

3. Search for a skill.

4. Tap **Enable to Use**, and follow any required account linking steps.

Once enabled, the skill is available on all your Alexa-compatible devices.

Productivity Hacks with Alexa

Beyond voice commands and entertainment, the Echo Dot can function as a digital productivity assistant. With the right settings and routines, Alexa can help you manage time, streamline tasks, and stay organized throughout your day.

Calendar and Scheduling

Alexa integrates with popular calendars such as Google Calendar, Microsoft Outlook, and Apple Calendar.

To connect your calendar:

1. Open the Alexa app.

2. Go to **More > Settings > Calendar & Email**.

3. Choose your provider and sign in.

Once linked, you can say:

- "Alexa, what's on my calendar today?"

- "Alexa, add a meeting with Sarah at 3 PM tomorrow."

- "Alexa, delete my 10 AM event."

Alexa can read daily schedules aloud each morning or as part of a routine, making it easy to stay on track.

Shopping and To-Do Lists

Alexa can maintain dynamic lists that sync with the Alexa app and can be accessed via phone or tablet.

- "Alexa, add milk to my shopping list."

- "Alexa, what's on my to-do list?"

- "Alexa, remove eggs from my shopping list."

For advanced list management, Alexa can integrate with apps like Todoist or Any.do.

Reminders and Time Management

Instead of setting reminders manually, use voice commands:

- "Alexa, remind me to send the report at 4 PM."

- "Alexa, remind me to water the plants every Saturday."

Reminders can be location-based (e.g., "Remind me to call Mom when I get home") if location services are enabled in the Alexa app.

Use timers to stay on schedule:

- "Alexa, set a timer for 25 minutes." (Ideal for Pomodoro technique)

- "Alexa, set a break timer for 5 minutes."

You can name timers for clarity:

- "Alexa, set a laundry timer for 40 minutes."

Notes and Quick Captures

If inspiration strikes or you need to jot something down hands-free:

- "Alexa, take a note."

- "Alexa, what are my notes?"

Although Alexa has limited native note-taking features, you can integrate with apps like Evernote via IFTTT (If This Then That) or third-party skills.

Daily Briefings and Flash Briefings

Create a daily flow of information with Alexa's Flash Briefing feature:

1. Go to **Settings > News** in the Alexa app.

2. Choose sources such as NPR, BBC, Reuters, or your local station.

3. Customize the order and content.

Then say:

- "Alexa, what's my Flash Briefing?"

- "Alexa, give me the news."

This combines news, weather, and traffic into one short, comprehensive summary.

Voice-Based Email Access

With Alexa's email feature, you can hear summaries of new messages:

- "Alexa, do I have any emails?"

- "Alexa, read my latest email."

To enable:

1. Go to **Settings > Calendar & Email**.

2. Link your email account and enable voice access.

Alexa will summarize emails by sender, subject, and timestamp. Note that full messages aren't read aloud unless explicitly configured.

Parental Controls and Kid-Friendly Settings

For households with children, Amazon provides a comprehensive suite of parental controls through **Amazon Kids** (formerly FreeTime), allowing parents to customize the Echo Dot experience to be age-appropriate, safe, and engaging.

Activating Amazon Kids on Echo Dot

To enable Amazon Kids:

1. Open the Alexa app.

2. Tap **Devices > Echo & Alexa**.

3. Select the Echo Dot you want to configure.

4. Tap **Amazon Kids** and toggle it **On**.

5. Create a child profile (name, age, etc.).

6. Choose allowed content and set usage restrictions.

Once Amazon Kids is active, Alexa will respond in a more kid-friendly tone and restrict access to adult content.

Features of Amazon Kids

- **Filtered Content**: Alexa blocks music with explicit lyrics and access to inappropriate skills.

- **Educational Content**: Children gain access to learning tools such as spelling practice, math quizzes, and educational podcasts.

- **Bedtime Controls**: Parents can restrict device usage during certain hours.

- **Time Limits**: Set daily usage caps for music, games, or skills.

- **Activity Reports**: View usage summaries in the **Parent Dashboard** at parents.amazon.com.

Amazon Kids also includes access to **Amazon Kids+**, a subscription service with curated content including audiobooks, games, and skills for children aged 3–12.

Kid-Friendly Commands

Here are examples of Alexa commands children can safely use:

- "Alexa, play a bedtime story."

- "Alexa, help me with my homework."

- "Alexa, play Disney music."

- "Alexa, tell me a dinosaur fact."

- "Alexa, what sound does a whale make?"

Many educational brands, including National Geographic, Nickelodeon, and Sesame Street, have custom Alexa skills for children.

Voice Recognition for Kids

Enable **Voice ID for Kids** to allow Alexa to distinguish your child's voice and automatically switch to kid-safe mode when recognized.

To set up:

1. Open the Alexa app.

2. Tap **Settings > Your Profile & Family**.

3. Add a child profile and train Alexa with voice samples.

This adds a layer of personalization and ensures Alexa delivers safe content even when other Echo devices are shared.

Communication Restrictions

Amazon Kids restricts communication features like calling and Drop In by default. Parents can choose to enable them only for approved contacts. This ensures safety and avoids unintended conversations.

To configure:

- Open the **Parent Dashboard** and approve specific contacts.

- Enable or disable calling, messaging, and announcements as needed.

Frequently Asked Questions

As the Amazon Echo Dot becomes a more integral part of the smart home ecosystem, users—especially new ones—often encounter questions about setup, features, privacy, performance, and integration. This chapter compiles the most frequently asked questions and provides accurate, user-friendly answers to help both beginners and experienced users resolve uncertainties quickly and confidently.

---

1. What is the difference between the Echo Dot and other Echo devices?

The **Echo Dot** is Amazon's most compact and affordable smart speaker. It provides core Alexa functionality in a smaller form factor, making it ideal for bedrooms, kitchens, and small rooms. In contrast:

- The **standard Echo** typically features improved audio quality and a larger speaker system.

- The **Echo Studio** is a high-end speaker with premium, immersive audio.

- The **Echo Show** models include a display screen for video calls, camera feeds, visual weather updates, and more.

The Echo Dot is best for users who want a basic, voice-first experience, while other models cater to those seeking better sound or visual interfaces.

2. Can I use Echo Dot without a smartphone?

You **need a smartphone or tablet** with the Alexa app installed for the initial setup. However, once the device is configured, you can operate most features entirely by voice without needing your phone again.

To adjust advanced settings, enable new skills, or manage routines, you will still need occasional access to the Alexa app on a mobile device.

3. Does the Echo Dot work without Wi-Fi?

No, the Echo Dot **requires an active Wi-Fi connection** to function properly. Alexa processes voice commands via Amazon's cloud servers. Without internet access, the device will not respond to most commands or deliver information.

Some Bluetooth functionality may still work for previously paired devices, but voice-based features and smart home controls will be unavailable offline.

---

4. How do I change the wake word?

To change the wake word from "Alexa" to something else:

1. Open the Alexa app.

2. Go to **Devices > Echo & Alexa**.

3. Select your Echo Dot device.

4. Tap **Wake Word**.

5. Choose from available options: **Alexa**, **Amazon**, **Echo**, or **Computer**.

Note: You cannot set a custom wake word beyond the predefined list.

---

5. Can Alexa understand multiple users?

Yes. Alexa can recognize **individual voices** through **Voice ID**. This allows Alexa to deliver personalized responses for:

- Calendar events

- Music preferences

- Call and message history

- Flash briefings

To set up Voice ID:

1. In the Alexa app, go to **More** > **Settings** > **Your Profile & Family**.

2. Tap **Voice ID** and follow the voice-training prompts.

Each household member should create their own profile and voice ID to enable personalization.

---

6. How do I stop Alexa from listening all the time?

While Alexa constantly listens for the wake word, it does **not record or send audio** until activated. However, you can disable the microphone entirely by:

- Pressing the **microphone off button** on top of the Echo Dot (this turns the LED ring red).

- Saying, "Alexa, stop listening." *(Note: This disables only some functions; full deactivation requires the button.)*

To manage recordings and privacy:

1. Open the Alexa app.

2. Go to **Settings** > **Alexa Privacy**.

3. Delete voice history, set auto-delete preferences, or disable voice recordings.

---

7. Can I use Alexa to make phone calls?

Yes. Alexa supports several types of communication:

- **Alexa-to-Alexa Calling**: Free calls between Echo devices or Alexa apps.

- **Phone Calling**: Make calls to mobile or landline numbers in supported regions (via mobile number registration).

- **Drop In**: Two-way audio communication between Echo devices.

- **Announcements**: One-way broadcasts to all devices.

To enable calling:

1. Open the Alexa app.

2. Go to **Communicate > Call**.

3. Grant access to contacts and verify your phone number.

Once set up, say: "Alexa, call [contact name]."

---

8. What can I do if Alexa doesn't understand me?

If Alexa mishears or misinterprets your commands:

- Make sure you are speaking clearly and at a moderate volume.

- Check for background noise or echo interference.

- Retrain Alexa using **Voice ID**.

- Try rephrasing the command.

You can also check your voice history in the Alexa app under **Alexa Privacy > Review Voice History** to see how Alexa interpreted your request.

---

9. How do I connect Echo Dot to Bluetooth speakers or headphones?

You can use your Echo Dot as a **Bluetooth input** (to stream to the Dot) or **output** (to stream from the Dot to external speakers).

To connect Bluetooth speakers:

1. Put your Bluetooth speaker in pairing mode.

2. Say, "Alexa, pair Bluetooth."

3. Open the Alexa app and go to **Devices > Echo & Alexa > [Device] > Bluetooth Devices**.

4. Select the device from the list.

To disconnect, say: "Alexa, disconnect."

---

10. Can I use Echo Dot as a speaker for my phone?

Yes. You can stream audio from your phone to the Echo Dot using Bluetooth.

1. Say, "Alexa, pair Bluetooth."

2. On your phone, go to **Bluetooth settings** and select your Echo Dot.

3. Play music or audio from your phone as usual.

Echo Dot will function as a standard Bluetooth speaker. Say "Alexa, disconnect" when done.

---

11. How secure is Alexa, and is my data safe?

Amazon has implemented **multiple security layers** for Alexa, including:

- Encrypted voice communication.

- Muting functionality with LED indicator.

- Auto-delete of voice history (optional).

- Restricted skill access controls.

You can review and delete voice recordings, disable skills, and manage device access at any time via:

Alexa App > Settings > Alexa Privacy

Amazon does not sell your personal data or use your voice for advertising. Still, users should regularly review privacy settings and limit unnecessary permissions.

---

12. Can I control smart home devices without using the Alexa app?

Yes. Once smart devices are paired with your Echo Dot and grouped appropriately, you can control them completely by voice.

For example:

- "Alexa, turn off the living room lights."

- "Alexa, set the thermostat to 72."

- "Alexa, lock the front door."

However, the Alexa app remains essential for:

- Device setup

- Renaming or grouping

- Routine creation

- Status monitoring

---

13. How do I manage music preferences and default services?

To set your preferred music service:

1. Open the Alexa app.

2. Go to **Settings > Music & Podcasts**.

3. Link services like Spotify, Apple Music, Amazon Music.

4. Tap **Default Services** and set your preferences.

Now, commands like "Alexa, play rock music" will automatically use your chosen service.

---

14. Can Alexa control multiple devices at once?

Yes. You can create **Groups** and **Routines** to manage multiple devices with a single command.

- **Groups**: Combine devices into rooms (e.g., Bedroom, Office) to issue group commands like "Alexa, turn off the bedroom."

- **Routines**: Combine multiple actions into a custom command such as "Alexa, good morning" to turn on lights, play music, and report the weather.

These tools allow for smarter, more personalized automation.

---

15. What do the colors on the Echo Dot mean?

The Echo Dot uses its LED ring to provide status feedback:

- **Blue**: Alexa is listening or processing your request.

- **Red**: Microphone is muted or camera disabled.

- **Orange**: Device is in setup mode or connecting to Wi-Fi.

- **Purple**: Do Not Disturb is active.

- **Yellow**: You have a notification or message.

- **Green**: Incoming call or active Drop In.

- **White**: Volume is being adjusted.

These indicators help you quickly understand what the device is doing at any given time.

---

16. Can I move my Echo Dot to another room?

Yes. Simply unplug the Echo Dot and plug it in elsewhere. It will reconnect to your Wi-Fi automatically, assuming your signal reaches the new location.

If needed, you can rename the device or assign it to a new group in the Alexa app: **Devices > Echo & Alexa > [Device] > Settings > Device Location/Group**

---

17. Do I need multiple Echo Dots for different rooms?

While one Echo Dot can control smart devices in the entire home, having multiple Dots allows for:

- Room-specific commands

- Better microphone coverage

- Multi-room music

- Intercom functionality (Drop In, Announcements)

Each device can be configured for a specific room or task. Amazon allows seamless syncing and communication between devices.

---

18. What happens if I change my Wi-Fi network?

If your Wi-Fi name or password changes, the Echo Dot will not reconnect until updated.

To change Wi-Fi settings:

1. Open the Alexa app.

2. Go to **Devices > Echo & Alexa > [Device]**.

3. Tap **Wi-Fi Network > Change**.

4. Follow on-screen instructions to reconnect.

You may need to reset the device to setup mode if connection fails.

---

19. How do I update my Echo Dot's software?

Updates are installed automatically when the Echo Dot is idle and connected to Wi-Fi.

To check manually:

- Say, "Alexa, check for software updates."

- Or unplug and replug the device to trigger a check.

There is no need to download updates manually. Keeping the device plugged in ensures it stays current.

---

20. Can Alexa help with language translation?

Yes. Alexa supports **real-time translation** between multiple languages.

Try:

- "Alexa, how do you say 'thank you' in French?"

- "Alexa, translate 'Where is the bathroom?' into Spanish."

For ongoing translation, use **Live Translation Mode**:

- Say, "Alexa, translate English to Italian."

- Speak normally, and Alexa will translate both sides of the conversation.

Conclusion and Recommendations

The Amazon Echo Dot is more than a compact speaker—it's a powerful digital assistant designed to simplify, automate, and enrich everyday living. Whether you're just beginning your smart home journey or expanding an existing ecosystem, understanding the full scope of the Echo Dot's capabilities is essential to maximizing its value.

In this final chapter, we will summarize the key takeaways from the previous sections, provide overarching guidance for long-term use, and offer strategic recommendations for optimizing your experience. With the right knowledge and consistent use, the Echo Dot becomes a truly indispensable tool in the modern home.

Summary of Key Points

Throughout this guide, we explored each aspect of the Echo Dot in detail. Below is a consolidated overview of the most important information you've learned.

What the Echo Dot Is

- The Echo Dot is a voice-controlled smart speaker powered by Amazon's Alexa voice assistant.

- It enables hands-free access to information, media, and smart home functions.

- It is compact, affordable, and designed for use in bedrooms, kitchens, offices, or as part of a larger smart home setup.

Setting Up the Echo Dot

- The unboxing experience is minimal, with just the device, power adapter, and quick start guide.

- Initial setup requires the Alexa app, available for iOS and Android devices.

- Once connected to Wi-Fi, Alexa becomes fully functional and ready to receive voice commands.

- The latest model includes design enhancements, a temperature sensor, faster responses, improved speaker performance, and Eero mesh network integration.

Using the Alexa App

- The Alexa app is essential for managing device settings, adding new devices, creating routines, and linking services.

- Users can personalize voice responses, configure notifications, adjust privacy controls, and manage smart home integrations.

- The app also supports multiple users, allowing for individual profiles, calendars, and preferences.

Everyday Voice Commands

- Alexa responds to a wide range of voice commands for checking weather, playing music, managing reminders, setting alarms, and answering general queries.

- You can control media playback, issue communication commands, and receive customized responses based on user profiles.

Timers, Alarms, and Reminders

- Alexa excels at time management: set named timers for cooking, multiple alarms for different days, and one-time or recurring reminders.

- Timers and alarms can be adjusted or canceled using simple voice commands.

Entertainment Features

- The Echo Dot supports music streaming from services like Amazon Music, Spotify, and Apple Music.

- Users can access podcasts, audiobooks via Audible, and live radio from TuneIn or iHeartRadio.

- News briefings and weather reports can be customized and included in morning routines.

Smart Home Control

- The Echo Dot serves as a control hub for compatible smart devices, including lights, plugs, thermostats, locks, cameras, and appliances.

- Users can group devices by room, create routines for multi-action triggers, and automate environments based on schedules or sensor inputs.

Advanced Capabilities

- **Routines**: Automate daily tasks by combining multiple actions into a single voice command or scheduled trigger.

- **Drop In and Announcements**: Enable in-home communication and one-way broadcasts across Echo devices.

- **Multi-room Audio**: Synchronize music across multiple Echo devices or create stereo pairs for enhanced sound quality.

- **Privacy Controls**: Disable microphones, manage voice recordings, review app permissions, and control data retention.

Troubleshooting and Maintenance

- Common issues—such as Wi-Fi disconnection, unresponsiveness, or sound problems—can often be resolved through simple troubleshooting steps.

- Resetting the device restores factory settings and is helpful when transferring ownership or resolving persistent errors.

- Keeping the Echo Dot up to date ensures continued compatibility, feature enhancements, and security patches.

Tips and Tricks

- Third-party skills extend Alexa's capabilities into areas like productivity, games, education, and health.

- Alexa can integrate with calendars, shopping lists, and to-do apps for seamless organization.

- Amazon Kids provides robust parental controls, kid-friendly skills, and content filtering for safe family use.

Frequently Asked Questions

- The FAQ section addressed common user concerns about privacy, connectivity, compatibility, performance, and more.

- Echo Dot users now have a reliable resource for resolving issues and optimizing device settings.

Final Thoughts on Maximizing Your Echo Dot Experience

With a broad understanding of how the Echo Dot works, the focus now turns to how best to incorporate the device into your daily life for maximum benefit. The tips and recommendations below serve as both a recap and a strategic guide for sustainable, effective use.

1. Think Beyond the Basics

While simple voice queries and media playback are the most common uses, Echo Dot is capable of much more. Explore its deeper functionality:

- Create complex routines to streamline mornings, commutes, or evening wind-down periods.

- Enable skills for niche interests—whether it's meditation, language learning, trivia, or personal finance.

- Use the Echo Dot as a control panel for a growing smart home infrastructure.

Taking the time to configure and experiment with lesser-known features transforms Alexa from a voice assistant into a fully integrated household companion.

2. Use Profiles and Voice IDs

If you share your Echo Dot with family members, set up individual profiles and enable **Voice ID**. This ensures that Alexa tailors responses to the correct person:

- Calendar reminders are sent to the right user.

- Playlists reflect personal preferences.

- Calls and messages stay personalized.

In multi-user households, personalization significantly enhances the experience.

3. Take Advantage of Automation

Automation is one of the Echo Dot's most powerful features. Use it to reduce repetitive tasks and simplify your routines:

- Automate lighting, heating, and music when arriving home or waking up.

- Schedule reminders and to-do lists to match your productivity flow.

- Combine multiple actions—like weather, traffic, and news briefings—into a single command for mornings.

The more routines and automations you configure, the more efficient and intelligent your daily operations become.

4. Leverage Multi-Room Functionality

If you own more than one Echo device, consider setting up **multi-room groups**. This allows for:

- Seamless music streaming across the house.

- Room-specific announcements.

- Intercom-style communication with Drop In.

Each Echo Dot becomes a node in a broader home audio and communication network.

5. Prioritize Privacy Settings

Amazon provides extensive tools to manage how Alexa interacts with your data. Visit the **Alexa Privacy Dashboard** regularly to:

- Review and delete voice recordings.

- Set data retention policies.

- Manage smart home history and permissions.

- Limit skill access to sensitive information.

Understanding and controlling these settings ensures that the Echo Dot remains secure, especially in shared environments.

6. Use Alexa as a Learning and Discovery Tool

Alexa's ability to access knowledge, definitions, historical facts, and real-time information makes it an excellent educational companion. Whether you're cooking, studying, or relaxing, Alexa can:

- Teach you a new word or phrase.

- Translate foreign languages.

- Offer insights into current events.

- Help with math or science problems.

Encourage children and adults alike to use Alexa as a hands-free research tool or learning assistant.

7. Update and Maintain Your Device

Routine maintenance is minimal but important:

- Keep your device plugged in and connected to Wi-Fi to receive automatic updates.

- Occasionally restart the Echo Dot for optimal performance.

- Clean the exterior with a dry cloth, especially in kitchen environments.

- Review smart home setups and device groups to ensure continued relevance.

Well-maintained devices experience fewer issues and offer consistently high performance.

8. Explore Voice-Controlled Accessibility

Alexa's hands-free interface is particularly valuable for users with mobility limitations or visual impairments. Features like voice timers, appliance control, and text-to-speech functionality can increase independence and comfort.

Consider enabling accessibility skills and customizing routines for specific needs, such as:

- Automated door locks

- Voice-activated emergency contact routines

- Timed light changes and motion-sensor triggers

The Echo Dot is not just convenient—it can be life-changing in accessibility-focused scenarios.

9. Keep Exploring

Alexa and the Echo Dot platform are constantly evolving. New skills, features, integrations, and devices are released regularly. Staying informed ensures you never miss an opportunity to improve your smart home experience.

To stay updated:

- Browse the **Skills & Games** section in the Alexa app.

- Enable **Alexa Updates** in your notification preferences.

- Read Amazon's official announcements and newsletters.

- Experiment with newly launched routines or third-party integrations.

Continual exploration leads to continual improvement.

Final Recommendation

The Echo Dot is most valuable when treated as a dynamic, evolving tool. It offers flexibility for both casual and advanced users, adapts to family environments, and supports everything from entertainment to productivity and automation.

To truly maximize your Echo Dot experience:

- Embrace customization.

- Integrate smart home devices gradually.

- Use routines to reduce friction in daily habits.

- Prioritize privacy management.

- Encourage all family members to contribute to routines, skills, and content preferences.

Used thoughtfully, the Echo Dot can enhance how you manage your time, connect with others, and enjoy your space.